Foundations of Christian Culture
Ivan Ilyin

translated by
Nicholas Kotar

Chapter One
The Crisis of Contemporary Culture

EVERYTHING THAT HAS occurred in the twentieth century, and continues today, is proof of the fact that Christianity in the world is suffering a serious religious crisis. Massive swathes of the population have lost their living faith and have left the Christian church. But, having left it, many have not remained indifferent to it. Many have become antagonistic, judgmental, and estranged from it. For some, the antagonism is passive and cold. But others organize a willful battle against it, though still adhering to the rules of war. Still others have a fanatical hatred toward Christianity, and sometimes this spills over into outright persecution.

However, the difference between all three is not profound, nor is it foundational. Taken together, they are a unified front of mutual agreement, empathy, and even support, whether open or secret.

Thus, within the limits of what was formerly Christendom (we leave aside other religions such as Buddhism, Islam, Hinduism, etc.), there is a wide anti-Christian front that has tried to create an un-Christian, even an anti-Christian, culture. This phenomenon is not a new one. The twentieth century, following in the footsteps of the nineteenth, only manifests a process that has been dormant, but developing, for centuries. The process of separation of culture from faith, religion, and the Church began a long time ago. It has been going on for several centuries. In Europe and America, "secular culture" and secularization itself can trace their beginnings all the way to the Renaissance.

During the first fifteen centuries after the birth of Christ, the situation was radically different. There could be many reasons for this. Possibly, people in general were more trusting, their spiritual makeup less complex and variegated, more instinctive, less rationalistic; therefore, they may have been more modest and spiritually careful. Perhaps the divine origin of the revelation of the Gospel was more immediately apparent, more vividly and profoundly experienced. Perhaps man did not yet feel himself to be a master of nature, but one subjected to its whims. Or maybe life on earth was more chaotic and more fraught with danger. However it may be, it was during this time period that people in general (in Christendom, I repeat) considered religion to be the center of their lives, the most important, or possibly even exclusive, source of existence and meaning.

For the last four centuries, and especially during the eighteenth and nineteenth centuries, all this radically changed. I am not at liberty to follow the complete historical process here—that is a difficult and detailed endeavor worthy of its proper treatment. Even the end of the Middle Ages contained within itself the forerunners and the beginnings of these changes. And we are the ones having to reap what they sowed.

European culture of the 19th century was in essence already secular and de-sacralized. Science, art, law, agriculture, worldview, cosmology—all of these were thoroughly secularized. The culture of our own time continues this separation from Christianity, but not only from Christianity. Contemporary culture is losing its religious spirit, its meaning, and its beauty. It has not turned to any "new religion," nor has it even started to seek anything of the sort.[1] Having separated from Christianity, it has gone into an a-religious, godless wasteland. Mankind has not only ceased to contemplate, develop, and preserve the experience of the Christian church, but it has brought fruit to no other religious experience at all. It has left Christianity, but wanders the wasteland aimlessly.

Beginning with the French Enlightenment (and the Revolution it spawned), the history of the nineteenth century is one of many attempts to build a spiritually rich culture outside "religious prejudices" and without any unnecessary hypotheses concerning metaphysics and the soul. Slowly, a faithless culture arose, one devoid of faith, God, Christ, and the Gospels. And the Church gradually found itself in the position of having to grapple with this "independent" new culture.

What ended up happening was a formation of a world-vision that was completely separate from a vision of God. Positive science made huge leaps; those leaps led to ever-increasing practical and technical improvements, leading even to social revolutions. All this, taken together, has so changed the makeup, striving, taste, and needs of the human soul, that the Christian church with its natural conservatism in teaching (dogmas!), organization (canon law!), and prayer (ritualism!) did not find enough creative initiative and flexibility within itself to preserve its previous authoritative position in questions of human knowledge and activity, in questions of cultural theory and practice.

As a result, modern man has continued to travel ever further away from the eternal truth of Christianity. We have lost our ability to contemplate these truths, we have habituated ourselves to live without them. And so, we have degenerated intellectually and morally, plunging ever closer to a complete culture crisis, unheard-of in the history of mankind.

This is what modern man seeks:

1) First, **materialist science.** This science bases its success on how much it furthers its "truths" from the "hypothesis of God," breaking nearly all links with any kind of religion. Positive naturalism, with its "proofs", immediately provides utility with every new finding. Too often, scientific breakthroughs lead to more effective and cruel methods of waging war. This is not science, but "technical knowledge" that has no interest in exalted goals or the meaning of life. It is constantly revealing something or achieving a breakthrough, but it exists in a vacuum of a-morality. It has no reference to any objective standard or any revelation from on high.

2) Second, **secular, a-religious politics.** Modern man doesn't understand that politics have been cut off from the highest goal, which is (and always has been and always will be) to prepare people for the "beautiful life" (Aristotle), for life "in God" (Augustine). Godless governments are like the blind leading the blind into a pit. They do not value the eternal, noble, Christian roots of legal consciousness. Modern governments don't prioritize quality of life or perfection of life. They serve private

interests, whether class interests or individual interests. Politics knows nothing about measuring spiritual depths. Even in the best cases, modern politics create a chaotic balance of competing desires. This is all politics can do to combat enmity and envy.

3) Third, modern man is governed by an instinct to obtain and consume. The laws of the market rule over him, and he has no power over these laws, because he has lost the sense of the presence of the Living God in his heart.

We have reached an absolute dead end of capitalist production and have found only one way out of it—socialism and communism. We have not understood that it isn't capitalism itself that's horrifying. It's a godless capitalist regime that is horrifying, because is it upheld by people who have dead souls. But godless communism is endlessly more horrifying than godless capitalism. And so, having lost both God and Christ, the soul of modern man, religiously chaotic and morally degenerate as it is becoming, cannot help but become a victim of the instinct to buy and buy and buy even more.

4) Fourth, modern man has abandoned himself to a-religious and godless art that is becoming nothing more than vain entertainment, an enervating and depressing spectacle. In all times and places, there has been a call for "bread and circuses." But the bread and circuses have never pretended to be high art. Now, however, so-called modern art, which has "freed" itself from religious feeling and nuance, dances hand in hand with the desires of the masses. There is no longer a distinction between high and low art. It's as though art has become two-dimensional, losing its artistry, sacredness, objectiveness. The two-dimensional soul can only produce two-dimensional art, remarkable only for its triteness, its lack of depth.

Is there a creative way out of this situation? How can we find it? Is a renewal of culture even possible? And how can we help bring it about?

Chapter Two
The Problem of Christian Culture

WE SHOULDN'T THINK that this crisis only belongs to the past, or that it's behind us. No, it's only beginning. Truly profound, sincere, and unified Christian religiosity will not be reborn so easily or quickly only because of confusion or fear. It will only be reborn from sincere sorrow at being estranged from God's bosom, only through love that is renewed through contemplation and wisdom. Seemingly, half the known world suffers from "enlightened atheism," and so it doesn't seek that love, nor does it even know how to seek it.

For such people, their own light is enough. They don't even stop to consider that true illumination is the light of God, which leads to God and reveals Him. And people will probably have to pay for this "enlightened atheism," which produced all the horrors of a brutal communist regime, because the creative potential and spiritual resilience of modern man have been undermined by his rootlessness.

And so, in the hottest moment of the conflagration that is the great spiritual and religious crisis of our time, we are faced with the problem of Christian culture.

How is Christian culture even possible today when the cultural elite runs away from Christianity and tries to lead along the uneducated or half-educated masses with them? How is Christian culture possible when Christianity has still not found a true and creative reconcilement and cooperation with the great secular powers that inspire people these days, that is, with science, art, the economy, and politics? Especially when a strange and frightening revolt is occurring in the human soul against faith and Christianity, that same bestial and unbridled instinct preached by Nietzsche.

It seems that humanity has only two paths from which to choose—either to create an un-Christian culture or to reject culture completely from Christian motives.

There is no doubt that un-Christian culture is possible for nations who have no Christian faith, such as the nations embracing Islam, Buddhism, Shintoism, etc. But nations who have long been Christian and who have lost that faith without obtaining any new faith can only make vain attempts at creating culture without faith and God, that is, "atheist culture." These attempts are foreordained to fail. Nothing will come of them, because culture is not created by the rational mind, nor by the force of will. It is created by a unified, prolonged, and inspired tension of a people's entire essence, seeking a beautiful form for profound content. This includes the unconscious powers of the soul and instinct first of all. But instinct is capable of holding and creative a form, of gestating profound ideas, of becoming inspired, of loving and preserving culture, only as much as it communes with spirituality through love and faith.

Faith is the spiritual language of the instinct. To lose faith means to plunge the instinct into dumbness and powerlessness, or, on the contrary, to unbridle it completely. Therefore, a person without faith either lives in estrangement from his own instinct, not yet completely devolved to a lack of spirit and lack of form (the West), or it has already capitulated to an unbridled, Nietzschean, animal instinct (Bolshevism). The former situation allows people only to create flat, depraved imitations. The latter forces the person to create only formless chaos, sickly chimeras, twisted nightmares made real. Neither one nor the other is culture, because culture begins where spiritual content seeks a true and unified form.

This is the fate of nations that have lost their true faith and have fallen into agnosticism and atheism. They reject their old, precious culture and create nothing in its place. They become historical nonentities, cursed to humiliation, decomposition, and debauchery when they accept their sickly and foul creations as a kind of "new word of a new culture."

So what is left for a Christian? To reject culture outright because of his Christian principles? To interpret Christianity in such a way that he denies its power to transform mankind's deeds, life, and fate? To decide that Christ did not come to save mankind, not to call sinners to repentance, not to convert them to new life, but to leave them to perish in blindness, debauchery, and decomposition?

We cannot accept this as true! This is an incorrect interpretation of Christianity's role in the world, making even the strictest Buddhism more optimistic and humanistic! This would mean a rejection or even perversion of the profound meaning of Christ's coming. It would mean ceasing being a Christian at all. For a Christian is not called to flee the world or mankind, to reject or curse it. He is called to bring the light of Christ's teaching into earthly life and to creatively reveal the gifts of the Holy Spirit in the fabric of this life. And this means that we must create a Christian culture on this earth.

Thus it seems that a Christian has nothing else left to do but to turn to the Holy Scriptures and find direct quotations about the form of this Christian culture, then to begin creating it. But is that true?

Well, the fact is that there are no direct, or almost no direct, indications concerning the form of this Christian culture. Neither will we find any specific requirements or rules or any ideal program that could answer those forces that are pulling people away from Christianity—science, art, the economy, and politics.

What does the New Testament have to say about the study of the natural world, or about the possibility of a science that is explicitly Christian? We know that there were wise magi who came to worship Christ (Matthew 2:1-12), but there was also a foolish magus, Simon, who thought it possible to buy grace for money (Acts 8:9-24), as well as yet another magician, Elymas, who was punished by Apostle Paul with blindness (Acts 13:8-11). We know that the official "scientists" of the Jewish Church (the scribes) deserved the wrath of Christ and a hard condemnation (Matthew 23, Luke 11:40-45, and others), that Apostle Paul was a learned polymath (2 Corinthians 11:6, Acts 26, 24), and that he advised that we "avoid the contradictions of what is falsely called knowledge" (1 Timothy 6:20). So what can we draw out of this concerning the science of our days? Can it be Christian?

Or, what do the books of the New Testament say concerning art or the possibility of Christian art? We remember what Christ said about the beauty of the lilies of the field and the source of that beauty ("for it is God who clothes them so," Matthew 6:28-30). But we also know that in Athens Paul was very upset when he saw the city filled with idols (Acts 17:16). We know what a terrible schism arose as a result of the problem of iconoclasm, and knowing all this, do we also not wonder how all this might apply to contemporary visual art, music, sculpture, or dance?

It seems more likely that there is some hope of finding more precise instructions concerning government and politics in the Bible. But what do we see? We know the words of Christ who said to the Pharisees, who were tempting Him, "render unto Caesar the things that are Caesar's, and to God the things that are God's" (Matthew 22:16-21). But we cannot fail to immediately ask the question: are we to understand that the things of Caesar are completely alien to godliness? Do godly actions, then, have nothing to do with government and politics? We know that Christ nowhere condemned the sword—not the sword of the government, nor the sword of the military; however, He did warn that "all who take the sword will perish by the sword" (Matthew 26:52). We remember that Pilate had authority given him from Above (John 19:11), and we know that Apostles Peter and Paul both called their followers to submit to earthly authorities, according to their conscience, for "there is no authority except from God" (Romans 13:1). But we also see that these words have different interpretations, and there have been (and continue to be) spiritual authorities that are ready to accept any usurper of power—even a thief or an atheist—as an "authority from God." And so we wonder: by what measure are we to be guided when we create Christian culture in a modern government?

And so on.

This is the difficulty for the modern Christian who is presented with the problem of Christian culture for a modern age—either he finds no direct quote from Scripture to guide him, or he finds such general axioms that can be interpreted in different ways and which have been interpreted differently by different Fathers of the Church. A detailed study of these commentaries throughout history can doubtless be of great interest to any Christian, but this requires significant educational preparation and still leaves the seeker either completely without an answer (especially concerning science) or with an answer so limited that he is forced to continue seeking, each to the measure of his own strength.

Chapter Three
The True Path

I would even venture to say that the entire history of Christianity is nothing other than a single, great search for Christian culture, beginning from the first apostolic times, starting with the descent of the Holy Spirit on the apostles, from the first healing of Apostle Peter (Acts 3), from the first Christian communities (Acts 4-5), and ending with the Pope's encyclical *Rerum Novarum* and the labors of the All-Russian Council of 1917-1918.

It is true that this search has resulted in some extreme teachings. Some are ready to reject earthly culture, or the world itself where we were created, in the name of Christ. Others are ready to assimilate too much earthly and worldly content, even going so far as losing the living Spirit of Christ. But the Christian Church has always striven to find a path between these two extremes. This is a kind of royal, wise path of life that brings Christ back into the world by rooting our existence in Christ and by creatively filling the fabric of human life with His light. This is the path to which anyone who thinks of creating a Christian culture must anchor his feet.

But for this, it is first necessary to overcome the temptation of rational formalism. What do I mean by that? We should never think that the Holy Scriptures of the Old or New Testament are a book of rules that contain within themselves certain rules for every circumstance of life and every difficulty. As though all a Christian has to do is deal with these rules and incorporate them into his life. Such ideas might be appropriate for a Judaic worldview or for a beginning lawyer, but they are completely inappropriate for a Christian worldview. It unfailingly will lead a person from a series of blindly-formulated questions to a series of blindly-formulated answers. It will lead every Christian to a literalist reading of the

Scriptures and to a moribund interpretation of it. But it will never lead him to a living creativity filled with the Spirit and with meaning.

Pointless also are any attempts to rationally or formally fill in the gaps of Scripture with strictures, like the many tracts of "moral theology" that have littered Christian literature thanks to the Jesuits. In such books, it seems that all of life is determined by correct rules and advice for following those rules. There is no room for the living Christian conscience, which is instead replaced by rational analysis and formal deduction that leads a person into temptation and confusion.

The Gospel is a book of faith, freedom, and conscience. It is not a book of rules and laws. One must read the Gospel and understand it with a living spirit, through the depth of your own faith, your own freedom and conscience, not formalist rationalism. The Gospel contains a certain grace-filled and free Spirit, and it must be accepted with one's own spirit. Not with the flat, sober, common-minded reasoning brain, but with one's own free, conscientious, and spiritual vision, one's own ability to contemplate with the heart and to believe through spiritual vision. Then it will become clear that the Gospel is not a book that ties a person down with rules, but a living source of love and vision that pours into the soul and awakens in it the most profound sources of personal spirituality. This source pours into us and frees us to a personal vision, to a decision-making process, and to creativity. The Gospel (literally, the "good news") was not written to turn a person into a frightened slave who constantly awaits punishments and who doesn't dare to create independently. Such a slave is useless to God and man both—he is not the one to create Christian culture.

Instead, the Gospel exists to give man freedom in the Spirit, not a freedom without spirit—that would be a blind and passionate fatalism, nor a spirituality without freedom—that would be a formalistic righteousness of absence of personality. No, freedom in the Spirit, that is, the gift of personally seeing the divine and to simultaneously walk a divine path—to remain wholly and willingly with one's own spirit in the Spirit of God. For "the Lord is the Spirit, and where the Spirit of God is, there is freedom." (2 Corinthians 3:17) Therefore, the Gospel gives us a perfect law, a law of freedom (James 1:25). It calls us and teaches us how to speak and how to act, how those people who are judged by the law of freedom speak and act (James 2:12). It instructs us to submit ourselves not as those who use freedom as a cloak for vice (1 Peter 2:16), but as free men, "for you, brethren, have been called to freedom" (Galatians 5:13).

The Spirit of Christianity is not literalistic, not pedantic, not regulatory, but renewing and freeing. To assimilate it, one must not interpret the words and texts in a legalistic manner, but by imbuing one's spirit with its spirit of love, faith, conscience, and freedom. This doesn't mean that the Gospels are not absolutely necessary. They are necessary, precious, just as Holy Tradition is. But one can learn the Scriptures by heart and be an expert in the Holy Tradition of the Church, and still not be renewed in a Christian manner.

To create Christian culture, we have to ourselves become renewed first, and only then take on the world with our hands. Furthermore, this taking on must be accomplished in the freedom of a perfect law. We see no other way out of it; most likely, there is no other way.

To renew ourselves evangelically—wholly, to our very depths—this is not given to everyone. But to start walking on this path, or at least try to step onto it—this is possible and necessary for all. In any case, it is for anyone who seriously thinks of Christian culture.

This renewal occurs thus. When reading the Holy Scriptures, the reader must not simply register what he reads with his mind, but he must try to find and confirm in himself that which is described in the text. If necessary, he must create that state from scratch. That is, he must try to evoke within himself the state of mercy and to dedicate himself to it, to contemplate God's perfection with the heart and to abide in it until the heart and the will (the action of the conscience) are filled with it, to find within oneself the power of love and to turn it (even for a moment) to God, mankind, and to all that is alive.

This is the beginning—the Christian approaches the casting off of the old man and the confirmation in the new. This new man will discover the true divinity of Christ. And all this must be accomplished in the heart and the soul, but not only in them; in the mind, but not only in the mind; by the will, but by action also; by faith, but by deeds as well. First and foremost, it is accomplished by active love.

In the Scriptures of the New Testament this renewal is described thus: "Let the word of Christ dwell in you richly in all wisdom" (Colossians 3:16), "and do not be conformed to this world, but be transformed by the renewing of your mind, that you may prove what is that good and acceptable and perfect will of God" (Romans 12:2), so that you can be "renewed in the spirit of your mind, and that you put on the new man who was created according to God, in true righteousness and holiness" (Ephesians 4:23-24), "that you may be filled with the knowledge of His will in all wisdom and spiritual understanding." (Colossians 1:9) "But above all these things put on love, which is the bond of perfection." (Colossians 3:14)

From this, according to the teaching of the Scriptures, a "pure mind" (2 Peter 3:1) in man not only comes alive, not only does "the peace of God, which surpasses all understanding" (Philippians 4:7) flow into him, but an essential, actual unity of the soul with Christ and God begins. For then God "grants you, according to the riches of His glory, to be strengthened with might through His spirit in the inner man, that Christ may dwell in your hearts through faith." (Ephesians 3:16-17) Then you will come "to know the love of Christ which surpasses knowledge, that you may be filled with all the fullness of God." (Ephesians 3:19) For "God is love, and he who abides in love abides in God, and God in him." (1 John 4:16) "Do you not know that you are the temple of God and that the Spirit of God dwells in you?" (1 Corinthians 3:16) So much so that "he who joins with the Lord is one spirit with Him." (1 Corinthians 6:17)

Thus, it is possible for man to have a grace-filled union with God and Christ on earth. He can become a partaker of the divine essence (2 Peter 1:4). This communion and union are what give him new creative strength.

In His final conversation with His disciples at the Mystical Supper, Christ promised His disciples the gracious gifts of the Holy Spirit: "I will pray the Father, and He will give you another Comforter, that He may abide with you forever—the Spirit of truth, whom the world cannot receive, because it neither sees Him nor knows Him; but you know Him, for He dwells with you and will be in you." (John 14:16-17) "The Comforter, the Holy Spirit, whom the Father will send in My name, He will teach you all things, and bring to your remembrance all things that I said to you." (John 14:26) "But when the Comforter comes, whom I shall send you from the Father, the Spirit of truth who proceeds from the Father, He will testify of Me." (John 15:26) "He will guide you into all truth." (16:13)

This promise the apostles understood literally, not metaphorically. They referred it not only to themselves (Acts 2) and to their disciples (Acts 4), but to all who accept Christ to be the Son of God through faith and love. For this was spoken concerning all, without limit, that "he who is joined to the Lord is one spirit with Him." Also, "As many as are led by the Spirit of God, these are sons of God." (Romans 8:14) And also: "Everyone who loves is born of God and knows God." (1 John 4:7) and "everyone who practices righteousness is born of Him." (1 John 2:29) The Holy Spirit is promised to all Christians who abide in Christ. Through Him is the love of Christ poured out into our hearts (Romans 5:5). He renews our mind and our reasoning, so that we can "retain God in [our] knowledge." (Romans 1:28) He lives in us, guides us, "bears witness with our spirit that we are children of God" (Romans 8:16) and in the hour of sincere prayer "Himself makes intercession for us with groaning which cannot be uttered." (Romans 8:26) When we abide in Him, we can act like children of the light and bear the fruits of the Spirit, which "is in all goodness, righteousness, and truth." (Ephesians 5:8-9) Then He "who is able [will] do exceedingly abundantly above all that we ask or think, according to the power that works in us." (Ephesians 3:20-21)

While accepting this apostolic teaching to be true, there is no need to interpret it in a way that would lead to some kind of pride, arrogance, violence against others, or even false prophecy. On the contrary, this path requires of a person complete, unfeigned, sincere humility, sobriety, laborious effort and asceticism—that is, all that is so fully revealed in the *Philokalia* and that is brought into most vivid life by the elders of our Church. This, of course, shows that only few can reach the heights of this path. But seeking this path and coming close to it—this is commanded to all, especially those who would creatively build Christian culture.

Christian culture can be one of two things. First, it can be a beautiful, but vague word that can cover or justify too many things; we do not speak of this here. Or it is a great and supremely difficult, imperative and conscientious action. Its essence is to take in, to the best of one's abilities, the Spirit of Christ, and with it to create earthly culture for mankind. To create, with boldness, taking responsibility for one's own decisions, thought processes, and actions, and yet always calling to the One Who "is able to do exceedingly abundantly above all that we ask or think." Whoever wants to create Christian culture must try to cultivate in his own heart a child of the light and to give it the freedom to act as is appropriate for a person who acts as though he is subject to the law of freedom.

I see no other way forward.

Chapter Four
The Foundation of Christian Culture

CULTURE is an inner, organic phenomenon—it grabs the most profound depths of the human soul and it comprises paths of living, even mystical, viability. In this way it is different from civilization, which can be assimilated externally and superficially, and doesn't require the fullness of spiritual participation. Therefore, a people can have an ancient and subtle spiritual culture, but in questions of external civilization (clothing, living spaces, infrastructure, industry, etc.) it can appear to be quite backward or primitive. The opposite is also true. A people can stand on the absolute high point of technology and civilization, while in the areas of spiritual culture (morality, science, art, politics, and economy) they can be undergoing a period of degradation.

From this difference alone it should be clear just how uniquely significant Christianity is in the history of human culture. It brought into human culture a new, grace-filled spirit. This spirit had to vivify and did vivify the very essence of culture, its true nature, its living soul. This spirit was brought miraculously into enemy territory, so to speak, into the Judea-Roman world, an atmosphere of rational thinking, abstracted laws, formalistic rites and rituals, a dying religion, a thirst for worldly power, and animalistic instincts. Culture could not be created in such an atmosphere; it could only decay. This way could only lead to death. And it's clear that the people who lived in this atmosphere (the Pharisees) and the civilization that bred this way of life (Rome) could not accept the grace-filled teaching of Christianity. They needed to remain people and establishments of this world, against whom all the apostolic writings were directed.

But it was exactly this spirt that people needed to adopt if they were to become Christian; and now more than ever the same is true if we are to create Christian culture. What is the essence of this spirit?

It seems that every Christian should not only be a bearer of this spirit, but should understand it with such powerful clarity that he should be able to answer the question without even thinking about it. Nevertheless, I will attempt to describe it briefly.

1. The spirit of Christianity is a spirit of "internalization." ("The Kingdom of God is within you," Luke 17:21). If this is true, then everything external, material, sensory in and of itself has no worth and cannot be justified before the face of God. This does not mean that it should be completely and finally thrown away, however. It's like an empty field (and what farmer would ever want to reject his field?) Or it's like a beautiful carafe for expensive wine (after all, what's the point of an empty vessel? But even fine wine needs a vessel!) Or it's a building that cannot remain uninhabited. The internal, the hidden, the spiritual content decides the worthiness of the external, the manifest, the physical.

In our time, this should be an essential truth of any culture, especially Christian culture. Thus, the moral state of a person is judged not by his material status and not by how externally useful he is, but by the internal state of his soul and heart. Thus, a work of art is artistic not when it is "effective" or "original" in its aesthetic form, but when it is true to its concealed and spiritual subject matter. Culture is created from within. It is the creation of the soul and spirit. This means that only a soul strengthened in a Christian manner can create Christian culture.

2. The spirit of Christianity is the spirit of love. "God is love" (John 4:8)

This means that Christ indicated that love was to be the final and unconditional fountainhead of all creativity, consequently, of all culture. For culture creates and confirms; it brings a kind of accepting and abiding "yes." Love is the first and most important ability—to accept, to confirm, and to create. In love, the lover spiritually unites and intertwines with the beloved; he takes it on through the power of artistically identifying with the beloved and emptying one's self-ness. He abandons part of himself to accept part of the beloved. Something new is created, like in marriage or childbirth—the creation of the new is creativity.

Moreover, love is opposed immediately to abstract rationalization, crude willfulness, cold imagination, and sensuality. But it is opposed in such a way that all these tendencies, when subjected to love and filled with it, are renewed and brought back to new life. A thought moved with love becomes the power of reason, it connects with the object of knowledge and leads to true knowledge. The will that is birthed from love becomes conscientious, a good will that can become the source of truly Christian, heroic actions. The imagination stops being cold, stops being a vain and apathetic game, comes alight with spiritual fire and begins truly to see and to create. While sensuality, which is too commonly equated with "love", doesn't deserve the name. However, if it is imbued with love, it ceases being passionate, primal possession by lust, and begins to bring into life the laws of the spirit.

This is why a Christian cannot believe in a culture without love. Love for God is for him a source of faith. He refuses to find pleasure in cold, pointless style-over-substance art, no matter how vivid or insistent.

3. The spirit of Christianity is a spirit of contemplation. It teaches us to look at what is invisible to the senses (see 2 Corinthians 4:18) and promises us that those who are pure in heart, who live in holiness, will see God face to face.

Christian faith comes alive in spiritual evidence that is experienced by the eye of the heart. This evidence is the work of divine revelation and the internal freedom of each individual person. Therefore, the work of faith is a work of free vision and it doesn't endure any pressure from without. To force faith through violence, fear, or the sword has always remained an anti-Christian temptation.

This means that each person has access to a special, unconstrained power of spiritual contemplation through the heart, which can actually see God and come to know all that is divine in the world. This power of vision is what Christianity has given and bequeathed to all human culture. This power is what gives insight into scientific breakthroughs. This is what creates all truly transcendent art. In and of itself this spiritual contemplation is nothing other than a turning in prayer toward God. Therefore, we may say that Christianity has bequeathed to all people the right to build a culture that comes from prayerful contemplation and that remains rooted in it.

4. Furthermore, the spirit of Christianity is a spirit of living creative content, not merely the form of it. This is not to say that the form isn't treasured, it is! But when the form becomes abstracted from meaning and an end in itself, bereft of the content that fills and sanctifies it, it should be cast aside. Only through this spirit can the form cease to be form alone, but becomes a living vessel to contain life, virtue, art, knowledge, and righteousness—the entire fullness and richness of a cultural life.

This is why all Christians should mistrust any work that is inspired by formalism or excessive adherence to an external law. Formalism perverts everything it touches. Both science and art die in its presence. Therefore, the formalization and mechanization of culture is contrary to a Christian spirit and is proof of its decadence. A Christian seeks not external form, but form filled with content. He doesn't seek a dead machine, but organic life in all its mystery and in all its sacramentality. He is thirsty for a form that is born from a profound, spiritually-filled content. He seeks that true form. He wants to be, not too seem to be. He is given freedom, not the constraints of legalism.

5. Finally, the spirit of Christianity is a spirit of perfection. "Be ye perfect, as your Father in Heaven is perfect." (Matthew 5:48)

This does not mean that a Christian considers himself to be perfect or at least "close to perfection" in essence—contrary to all sobriety and humility. No, rather this means that a Christian has before his spiritual gaze the perfection of the divine, and he measures all earthly actions and circumstances by that standard. He learns to differentiate what is pleasant, what gives satisfaction or usefulness from that which is truly good, that which is objectively perfect. When he learns to differentiate between these two, he can attach himself to the more perfect, to prefer it, to achieve it, to serve it, to preserve it, even to die for it if necessary. A Christian not only contemplates Perfection, but recognizes his own inner need to strive for self-perfection. This leads him to have a vivid experience of his personal sinfulness and deficiency. He condemns himself, repents, and is purified. In every deed, he seeks the perfect and calls himself to it.

This is why Christianity is filled with a spirit of responsibility, self-condemnation, repentance, a spirit of diligence, conscientiousness, work, self-restraint, discipline, even asceticism. And this is why Christian culture is only possible if it comes from such a spirit and such an internal disposition. Any presence of the opposite spirit is proof of the distancing of culture from Christianity.

This is the spirit of Christianity that is given and bequeathed to human culture. This is the spirit of internalization, love, prayerful contemplation. A spirit of living, organic content; a spirit of sincere and profound form; a spirit of perfection and service to God through earthly matter. To believe in Christ means to take from the Son of God this spirit as the spirit of creative power and with it to create earthly culture. Whoever is true to this spirit, who creates and lives in it, he is Christ's, even when he doesn't know it or admit it! For everyone who practices righteousness is born of Him.

To create Christian culture does not mean to be legalistic concering abstract dogma or to force yourself to think only of things that are hidden from earthly eyes. It doesn't mean to refuse to freely contemplate, or to create only by the rules given by representatives of the earthly church. But it does mean to reveal the depth of your own heart for Christ's Spirit, and from Him to turn to a contemplative acceptance of God and God's world, as well as God's providential actions concerning the redemption of the world. For such a contemplative and active man is given the power to bring a Christian spirit to everything that he begins to do, including art.

However, to do this, he has to accept God's world and live in it.

Chapter Five
To Accept the World

WHOEVER WANTS TO CREATE Christian culture must accept Christianity, he must breathe it into the depth of his soul and turn back to the world with a new wholeness and freedom. Expressing myself in philosophical language, I oddly say that such a person is called to actualize within himself the religious "act" of Christianity, and from it to begin the creative work of transfiguring the world itself in a new spirit. Naturally, in order to do this, he must first accept the world created by God and given to us as a gift.

We know that in the history of the Christian church, there is an ancient tradition of rejection of the world (by this I do not mean monasticism, concerning which I will speak later, but an almost Buddhist strain of thought that rejects not only the sinfulness of the personal soul and its expressions in the eternal world, but the very thing we call "world"). Whoever followed this tradition seemed to be justified in not getting involved in the fate of the world or earthly humanity.

It was as though he was justified to go his own way and let people go where they will—even to perdition, to destruction, and to debauchery, into the power of the Serpent who deludes the nations (Revelation 20:3, 7). But he can only find such a justification if he himself accepts the responsibilities that flow out of such a rejection of the world—that is, if he actually quenched all that is earthly and human within himself and lived the rest of his days as though he were no longer present on earth, concentrating solely on imminent death, in the form (almost) of a bodiless spirit.

Truly, there was such an ancient tradition that rejected the world outright. This tradition was born from the eschatological passages of the New Testament, especially the Gospels and the Revelation. It became more widespread under the influence of certain Greek philosophical movements (Stoic and Neo-Platonic). Then, it reached an extreme form (such as the purported self-sterilization of Origen) under the influence of a formalistic, externally-focused legalism similar to Judaism. However, this tradition never expressed a complete or profound reference point of Christianity to God's world. It would be extremely instructive to do a detailed analysis of the presence of Platonic and Stoic abhorrence for, and rejection of, matter in Christian ascetic literature, because it coexisted with the Christian teaching of the grace-filled harmony of the world and the role of Providence in governing it, as well as the teaching of God's omnipresence (which sometimes even approaches dangerously close to pantheism!). Before our gaze, we see two different, sometimes seemingly incompatible worldviews. It's as though they stand next to each other, without pushing each other out, whispering to humanity two ways of living: rejection of the world and acceptance of the world.

The first path was conscientiously explored and experienced in the first centuries of Christianity. According to this worldview, the kingdom of God is not only not *of* this world, but not *for* this world. The external world of the senses is only a temporary and difficult prison for the Christian soul; it has nothing to do with this world, for which it has no calling, nor any creative work. The world and God are opposites. The laws of the world and the laws of the spirit are incompatible. You cannot serve two lords, and the lord of this world is the devil. This world and the world to come are two mortal enemies.

In this worldview, the purpose of Christianity is to flee *from the world*, that is, through the extreme putting down of earthly human nature. A Christian has to hate all that is worldly and to separate it from himself, otherwise it will separate him from God. All earthly good things, all that is created has to be considered foreign. He must not desire any of this.

The Christian, then, should avoid the marriage state, he has no right to private property, nor should he serve his government. Moreover, he should go so far as to pray constantly that this world pass away and that its days be shortened. As for himself, he must condemn his flesh to slow death for fear of being deprived of the final blessing at the end. He should be ashamed of the fact that he has a body and bodily needs. He should come to see his flesh as an enemy and to abhor it. A healthy body should be a something undesirable; it should stand on the earth as though it were nothing but a sculpture, and he should live as though he were completely not in this world.[2]

But what can a Christian do in such a world? What sort of culture can he create? What does he have to battle for in this world? If Christ came to the world, taught, and suffered to lead his disciples away from the world and teach abhorrence to all earthly matter, then the very idea of Christian culture is false and impossible. Such a Christian truly has no homeland on this earth, for it is already in the heavens. What sort of care can such hermit have for laws, for proper order, for justice or fairness? Why would a stylite be sad about the death of good science and the fact that museums are burning? With Tertullian, he is called to hate the world and think of death…

And if Christianity thus rejects the world, that is, matter, nature, the body, economics, private property, government, science, art, and all other such things, then it cannot lead mankind in <u>this world</u>. It can only lead mankind <u>out of this world</u>. To bless it for earthly life and to inspire us to bless this earthly life—such a Christianity is incapable of this. If this is so, then earthly life is not given to mankind so that he would live and create, glorifying God by his life and his creativity (the very idea of Christian culture) but so that he would not accept it and teach himself a slow self-mortification. A true Christian, then, has no creative calling or goal on this earth.

And when you cast a cursory glance over the cultural history of mankind for the last centuries and see this process of a mass exodus from the Church and Christianity, then sometimes I can't help ask myself if this process is not at least partially explained (in addition to the aforementioned spiritual crisis) by the fact that Christianity has not yet completely defeated this world-rejecting strain within itself, the one that teaches us to penitently leave the world, but does not teach us to enter conscientiously into the world and to joyfully create within it for the glory of God?

If we turn to the earliest manuscripts of the New Testament and examine them thoroughly, we are forced to conclude that the term "world" has several different meanings, and the very problem of rejecting or accepting the world must be resolved in different ways. Sometimes, the world means all of creation taken as a whole, as created by God Himself (see Romans 1:20, Ephesians 1:4, and others). Sometimes, the "world" is the unity of all nations to whom Christians must preach the Gospel (see especially the Great Commission in Matthew 28). It is very unlikely that Christ taught us to reject God's creation or the unity of all nations who desire the good news and who can receive it. Even this simple juxtaposition of several passages should illustrate just how carefully we should approach this problem. What is the "world" that is rejected by the New Testament?

In the Gospels and Epistles, the "world" is only rejected insofar as it has itself fallen away from God, standing in opposition to Him as something independent of Him and foreign to Him. This is the world that finds the confirmation of its values and reality without God and against God. This is the world that tempts and deludes mankind by awakening man's fallen sensuality (see Mark 4:19 2 Peter 2:20, Timothy 4:10, and others) and leading him to Satan. Insofar as the world "lies under the sway of the wicked one" (1 John 5:19) and is subjected to the prince of this world (see John 12:31), any friendship with this kind of "world" is against God, and "whoever wants to be a friend of the world makes himself an enemy of God." (James 4:4)

A Christian cannot and must not love such a world. "Do not love the world or the things in the world. If anyone loves the world, the love of the Father is not in him. For all that is in the world—the lust of the flesh, the lust of the eyes, and the pride of life, is not of the Father but of the world... And the world is passing away, and the lust of it, but he who does the will of God abides forever." (1 John 2:15, 17). Such a world cannot know God (John 1:10, 17, 25); it hates Christ and His disciples (John 7:7); it accepts and acknowledges its own (John 15:19).

But Christ has defeated the world (John 16:33), and "whatever is born of God overcomes the world. And this is the victory that has overcome the world—our faith." (1 John 5:4) Everything this world considers foolish, weak, ignoble, humiliating can actually be, before God's face, worthy and chosen (see 1 Corinthians 1:27). This world has its fallen joys and its own, dangerous sorrow (2 Corinthians 7:10). Its form is passing away, the faithful must not become attached to it, for temptations exist in it, to which "people of this world" abandon themselves (Luke 12:30). And they will be judged and condemned together with the world (1 Corinthians 11:32).

This sort of "rejection of the world" cannot possibly be interpreted as hatred of the matter created by God or as an essential failure of the earthly in human nature.

The cosmos was created by God—the heavens, the earth, the sea, and all that is in them. God is the Lord of heaven and earth (see Matthew 11:25). "For by Him all things were created that are in heaven and that are on earth, visible and invisible...And He is before all things, and in Him all things consist." (Colossians 1:16-17) Thus, His "eternal power and Godhead" are clearly obvious "since the creation of the world" "being understood through the things that are made" (Romans 1:20). This world must not be rejected out of hand.

But this refers to mankind as well, and even more so. Mankind was not rejected by God, and therefore we cannot reject mankind either. On the contrary, God saves and illumines mankind. "For God so loved the world that He gave His only begotten Son, that whoever believes in Him should not perish, but have everlasting life." (John 3:16) This is only one among many such quotes that demonstrate the power of Christ's incarnation and His desire to save all mankind.

All this means that the world may be rejected only insofar as it is not in God or against God, not in Christ or against Christ, insofar as it is a source or weapon of godless lusts. And the world must be accepted as created by God and having received from God its own meaning and its own calling, which is encapsulated in the incarnation that sanctified not man alone, but through man, all of creation. The meaning of this is expressed by these phrases: "I have overcome the world" John 16:33) And therefore "All authority has been given to Me in heaven and on earth." (Matthew 28:18) and "All things have been delivered to Me by My Father." (Matthew 11:27) And the calling of the world is as follows: "that in the dispensation of the fullness of the times He may gather together in one all things in Christ, both which are in heaven and which are on earth—in Him." (Ephesians 1:10)

This is the purpose and the justification for Christian culture.

This rich and profound tradition of Christianity didn't stop with the rejection of the God-created world and interpreted Christ's teachings in a different sense. It gave to asceticism a specific meaning—the precious means by which we purify our souls and free them. The Church worked out an entire system of spiritual purification—monasticism. According to this system, asceticism is a path that leads to knowledge of God both in heaven and on earth. Rejection of the world is not the essential and final task of the Christian. On the contrary, Christianity took on the world, blessed mankind in the world and began to teach him not only a Christian ending to our life, but Christian life itself, including creative work.

What else can we do except take on the world when it was created by God, loved by Him, saved, illumined, redeemed, and given to the authority of Christ, the Son of God? When God, who required nothing good for Himself, created the heavens and the earth for mankind, giving through them the pleasure of many good things? Where in the world is there a single place which Providence does not touch, where God is not, so that the one who wishes to see Him need only to look at the good order of everything and His Providence for all? (These are paraphrases of St. Anthony the Great, the father of monasticism) And this entire created nature is nothing other than a great book, in which man can read the words of God whenever he wishes (Evagrius the Monk)? When the Christian is given the great task not only of preaching Christ in all the world, but to inspire everything earthly with His Spirit?

Truly, Christ Himself accepted the world and was incarnate, not to teach us to reject the world, to abhor the creation of God, but to give us the chance and to show us the true path toward faithful, Christian "world-acceptance". To teach us to faithfully accept and creatively bear the burden of materiality and the burden of human separation and individuality, to teach us to live on the earth in the light of the kingdom of God. We are not greater than Christ, and Christ accepted an earthly life and returned it to us shining in His grace. And whoever accepts the world becomes a creator, taking on this world as part of his life's journey; that is, he assumes the task of the perfecting of self, neighbor, and matter itself through his spirit.

This is also the essence of Christian culture.

Man, by his nature, (and that means "from God") is given a certain form of earthly life. From the various circumstances flowing from this earthly life, we are given many inescapable tasks and responsibilities that we must accept, sanctify, and illumine with the light of Christian revelation. Practically, this means a life of labor, danger, even suffering, as we approach the divine and overcome that which is contrary to the divine. By His incarnation ,Christ did not reject this way of life, but accepted it and overcame it. And we must follow His footsteps and do His work, since it is the will of the Father, but not by the "oldness of the letter", but in freedom and "newness of the Spirit."(Romans 7:6)

This means that we must accept the lilies of the field, the birds of the air, pastorship, carpentry, even the ass; gold and frankincense and myrrh; bread, fish, and wine, and the joy of the wedding feast; tithes, both to the Church and to the state, the authority of Pilate, given to him from above, and whips against those who buy and sell in the temple; fear and trembling before the old and authoritative word, but also the singing of angels that brings news of the divine to us mortals. We must accept all of this as a gift and a task, as a Christian means leading to a Christian goal; as a creative life that can create a Christian culture. And to accept all this, we must do it "as free, yet not using the freedom as a cloak for vice, but as bondservants of God." (1 Peter 2:16)

In the first centuries AD, it was often thought that we had to accept Christ, but reject the world. The "civilized elite" of our time accepts the world and rejects Christ. But in the middle ages, the West offered yet another temptation—to preserve the name of Christ but to combine the spirit of His teachings, adulterated with the legalism of Judaism, with a cunning and power-hungry acceptance of a world not transfigured by Christ.

The best way out of all these situations is to accept the world as a consequence of accepting Christ, and to build Christian culture on top of that edifice. Thus, flowing from the Spirit of Christ, we may bless, give meaning to, and creatively transfigure the world, not condemning its external forms and laws, nor debilitating its spiritual power, but overcoming it all, transfiguring it, and beautifully give it form through love, will, thought, labor, creativity, and inspiration.

This is the very idea of Orthodox Christianity.

The essential purpose of Christianity in this sphere is to sanctify every moment of earthly toil and suffering, from baptism to the funeral service, in the prayers before the beginning of school, in the call of the peasant to send rain to the suffering earth during drought, in the blessing of wheat, wine, and oil, and in all the sacraments especially.

The Kingdom of Christ is not of this world (John 18:36); however, the world and mankind were saved by Him, and so the idea of the Kingdom is *for this world*, as its calling and promise. It is incorrect to think that the Kingdom of God is like earthly kingdoms. It is equally incorrect to think that it exists *for this world*. But this world exists as a great field (see Matthew 13:38) for the sowing and for the growth of the Kingdom of God. The Gospels' good news do not consist in the fact that earth and heaven are at odds or can never be joined, for the earth is condemned by sin and people are the children of that sin, but rather in the fact that heaven has already come down to earth in the person of the God-Man, that "the Kingdom of Heaven is at hand" (Matthew 4:17). There is a real and permissible acceptance of the world possible, even a transfiguration of the world. This is promised to us. *The Gospels bring to the world not a curse, but a promise, and to man not death, but salvation and joy.* It teaches not flight from the world, but the Christianization of the world. Therefore, Christian rejection of the world can be the soul-purifying life of a monk who rejects so that he can find anew, who closes his eyes so that he can come to see with spiritual vision, who seeks solitude and concentration to come to know God, man, and the world anew. In such cases, the Christian rejects not God's world as an objective reality, but his passions and the passionate content of his experience. Then, having been purified and illumined, he comes to see that there is "nothing unclean of itself, but to him who considers anything to be unclean, to him it is unclean." (Romans 14:14) Any other rejection of the world is blindness, a darkened spirit, something approaching blasphemy and heresy. It is a path from spiritual sterility to physical self-mutilation.

And so. Science, art, government, economics—these are, as it were, those spiritual hands by which mankind takes the world. And the task of the Christian is not to brutally chop off those hands, but to imbue their work from within through a living spirit accepted from Christ. Christianity has in this world a great task of the will, which many never accomplish. This task can be characterized as the creation of a Christian culture.

Today, when the pernicious phenomena of atheistic science, godless government, spirit-less art fill God's earth like a foul stench, Christians can neither turn away from it all, call themselves neutral, or hide behind their so-called rejection of the world. On the contrary, they must find inside themselves the faith and the will for sincere, creative, Christian world-acceptance and for a battle for their own field and their own crops. Then, healing may begin.

Chapter Six
Conclusion

THE creation of a Christian culture is a task placed before humanity at large two thousand years ago, and it has not yet been finished. This task cannot be finished by any single age, any single people, any generation, for every age and generation must strive to accomplish this task in their own way, even if that means that they fail in their own way. To become imbued with the spirit of Christ's teaching and to pour out that spirit into your life and into the physical world—this is our task, and it reveals an immense inner freedom and magnificent creative expanse before us.

Clearly, those who have striven and come before us, their spiritual labors remain precious and unforgettable treasures in the history of Christian culture. This means that the physical form of the things they created must be treasured and must be preserved for posterity. Everything touched by the Spirit of Christ becomes part of Christian culture and its history; the present is illumined by the past, which continues to teach and lead people. But this is not enough. After all, the light of Christianity must not merely illumine the life of other Christians, but the life of unchristian nations as well. This is why everything pure, profound, noble, and beautiful that has ever appeared on earth is considered by us Christians as familiar in spirit to us, even if it wasn't created by a Christian.

Such beauty is truly great and precious, for it was inspired by the power of the Lord in Whom we believe, even though He had not yet revealed Himself to that artist's consciousness, but mystically worked on the human heart. This is why we value Confucius, Lao-Tse, the Buddha, Zoroaster, Amenhotep IV, Heraclitus, Socrates and Plato, Marcus Aurelius and Seneca, Greek and Egyptian art, even the self-sacrificial patriotism of the Inca or the Japanese. Everywhere where people lived in creative love or gave their lives for another or prayed to God with groanings that cannot be uttered—here we sense with our spirit the Spirit of our Teacher and we see the universal brotherhood possible only in Christ.

This means that we do not imagine that the next generation of people can or must "create Christian culture". Not "create," but once again to step on the path of that creation, to return to it and renew this process, which has been historically interrupted. In other words, we must renew the Christian spirit and action within ourselves first, then bring it to our creativity in the world.

Furthermore, I do not think that the current secular and un-Christian culture should be entirely rejected or condemned out of hand. However, it should be revisited creatively, then renewed in the transfigurative spirit of Christianity. This doesn't mean, however, that science should start to include canon laws in its working hypotheses and theories, nor that art will become nothing more than traditional iconography and sacred architecture. To think like this would mean to fall prey to literalist legalism, which only destroys. It would also mean forgetting the essential axiom of Christianity, which is that every perfection begins with the heart and is accomplished in spiritual freedom. Neither the Church nor the government can nor should prescribe how the process of Christian cultural renewal should take place. It must be done freely. Of course, it does have to occur within the limits of the Church itself, and only later be handed off to the rest of the world.

This is how I imagine today's Christian culture to be created—the hearts of people that have already been shaken to their core by the current and coming calamities that have arisen thanks to atheism and anti-Christianity, will begin freely to return to the contemplation of Christ and to the bringing of the gifts of His Spirit back to life and culture. I cannot foretell when this will begin and how it will occur, I can only demonstrate the desirability and possibility of this difficult and lengthy task.

Whoever imagines, or better yet, fully experiences, the foundations and sources of Christian culture that I have enumerated, will see what a great and majestic spiritual expanse lies before modern man. The problem of Christian culture has not been resolved, and it will continue to be worked on by future centuries and their generations. Every one of us is called to enter the spiritual gates that Christianity has opened, though this call preserves our will and free choice—to enter or not to enter. For the last three hundred years, European culture has stopped at the threshold of these gates, turned away from them, and tried to create new paths. All of our culture is still dealing with the fruits of that turning away.

These fruits and consequences are expressed in the fact that the grace-filled spirit of Christianity began to abandon the world's high culture. People gradually transferred the purpose and meaning of their lives from the internal world to the external—matter became most important, and spirituality stopped being valued. Everything was reduced to the earthly—the heavenly realm stopped attracting eyes and hearts. Machines lord over organic matter. The rational mind exiled contemplation, prayer, and faith from the cultural space, attempting to compromise them. The content of life became unimportant; everyone ran the race to the bottom, chasing after the empty form.

Because of this, philosophy became nothing more than empty, formal abstraction. The scientific method pushed out exploration; style for style's sake became the norm in art, its content was declared unimportant. Modern man is little more than a flat, self-satisfied utilitarian. And so, his culture is equally so.

I don't know when mankind will begin turning away from this reality. But when they will, they will see a truly profound and majestic expanse open up before them—the reality of Christian culture. Before them will appear an entire series of important tasks, including the creation of Christian culture and art. This does not mean destroying all that came before, but creatively transforming it all through the profound depths of a transfigured and free spirit. Secular culture will not be destroyed, then, but will be transfigured and given spiritual depths through free contemplation, the spirit of love, the spirit of organic, sincere form, through a will toward objective perfection.

The best hearts of our time are sensing the beginnings of this process. And so I am comforted by this foreshadowing, there is hope in it that the Lord will not yet be wrathful with us "unto the end."

[1]. Written in 1937, this essay is somewhat limited in its applicability to the 21st century. The rise of the intellectual dark web, New Age spirituality, and what Charles Taylor calls "secular 3" does entail a kind of search for spiritual meaning. However, it is chaotic and completely devoid of a unified system of meaning or significance.

[2]. These ideas, expressed with some of the language of the primary sources intact, is found in such ancient Christian texts as the *Didache, Clement's Second Epistle to the Romans, The Sherpherd of Hermas*, as well as in the writings of some Montanists, Tatian, Origen, and others. We see hints of this in the later ascetic tradition of the Egyptian desert.

www.ingramcontent.com/pod-product-compliance
Lightning Source LLC
Chambersburg PA
CBHW060346080526
44583CB00014B/1075